CONTENTS

Executive Summary

In 2004, upon the request of His Majesty King Abdullah II, an initiative was launched to draft recommendations for the leadership in Jordan to advance the Kingdom's biotechnology sector, attracting global recognition, regional leadership, and capitalizing on the strengths and competitive advantages of Jordan's research universities, healthcare institutions and industries.

Dr. Samir Khleif, Director General and CEO of the King Hussein Cancer Center, led a steering committee which evaluated the capabilities of Jordan and implemented an aggressive action plan. This action plan provided a framework involving execution of short, intermediate, and long-term objectives of advancing the sector. An ongoing initiative on the development of Best Practices for the legal and regulatory framework, is being conducted by the Research Triangle Institute (RTI).

Three years later, Bearing Point contracted Biotech Compass to evaluate the status of the sector by reviewing existing data and publications, conducting interviews, evaluating biotechnology programs within the academic sector and assess the status of regulatory and Intellectual Property Rights. A set of recommendations are provided to USAID-SABEQ in which to take action in supporting the productivity of the sector.

Biotechnology offers solutions to global challenges from healthcare drug diagnosing and innovative medicines, to efficient agriculture usage and new energy modalities. When developing countries explore creating an ecosystem which supports the advancement of science and technology, initial questions regarding the status of their academic institutions, regulatory infrastructure and protection of Intellectual Property are raised. With the former USAID program, AMIR, a number of these challenges were addressed due to the accession of Jordan to the WTO and the US-Jordan Free Trade Agreement.

To date, in the public sector, there are a number of initiatives underway in the development of the biotechnology sector within the Kingdom of Jordan. His Majesty King Abdullah II launched a series of committees and numerous biotechnology programs within the academic institutions, including a National Biotechnology Center supporting incubator companies, and an analysis of the regulatory and legal infrastructure, and policy recommendations. The initial challenge identified with all of these activities is the lack of communication, integration, and follow through for existing programs. The funding mechanism that supports research collaboration amongst biotechnology programs in the Universities and linking them internationally would be a great asset. Creating a forum in which the private sector can identify resources in the Universities, whether human or technology, and then using these resources for the profitability and advancement of the sector. SABEQ now has the opportunity to transition this fledgling biotechnology industry, implementing certain components of King Abdullah II's existing action plan, and develop Jordan into a globally recognized regional leader for the advancement of the sector.

Background

Developing countries are far behind in their biotechnology industry and the role it occupies in their economies. Theses countries often find it difficult to direct their national strategies towards building the infrastructure necessary to nurture biotechnology or even to maintain existent research institutions that can support the broad demands of this sector. In many countries, this is due to a diminutive economy and lack of private sector involvement, which limits the resource base upon which to build a viable, productive research system; the core to biotechnology.

Commitment to building the biotechnology sector in countries with limited resources should stem from the great prospects of biotechnology-based industries. Lessons learned from developed countries as well as from some of the leading developing countries like Singapore, Ireland, Korea and Brazil, prove that biotechnology can create new high value employment, generate health and environmental benefits, and provide a strong basis for continued economic growth.

To catch up, the Arab countries need to invest heavily in both financial and human resources, to encourage private sector involvement within the academic institutions, motivate national, regional and international scientific cooperation and to benefit from the lessons of the advanced and newly active Science & Technology developmental nations. Strategic planning focused on how best to develop innovative products, build fast growing enterprises, create high value employment and attract international investment, all of which are powerful boosters of the economy.

Jordan's strategic location and welcoming investment opportunity is an important player in the Middle East. Jordan is a developing country with educated and English speaking manpower. Jordanian Universities, specifically the Jordan University of Science and Technology, offer undergraduate and graduate programs in biotechnology. Moreover, Jordanians are actively involved in technology transfer and know-how applications at the regional and international levels. Jordanian graduates are leaving Jordan to work in the biotechnology industry in India and the UAE. In conversations with Jordanian pharmaceutical manufacturers that are entering the international biotechnology industry, the one comment is that although these individuals are educated, the learning curve in which to transition them into specialty fields within the biotechnology industry is steep. This again highlights the segmented biotechnology programs within the Universities which have a shortage of funding dedicated to research.

Biotechnology Applications

In medicine, the utilization of transgenic microorganisms, animals or plants to produce biopharmaceuticals, monoclonal antibody-based, and nucleic acid-based medicinal products, now represent approximately one in every four genuinely new pharmaceuticals coming on the market. For such biopharmaceuticals, advances in the alternative production systems and delivery methods will have an important impact upon the number of commercial approvals over the remainder of this decade. Furthermore, pioneering stem research is opening ventures for the generation of tissues to replace injured or damaged ones. In addition, the development of molecular vaccines against infectious diseases as well as gene therapy targeted to correct genetic deficiencies. New diagnostic tools of biotechnology including antibody-based techniques and related tools of genomics and proteomics are in development.

In the agriculture biotech area, functional genomics including gene mining and their applications are on high demand for industry. Among which, is the generation of genetically modified (GMO) plants that withstand biotic and abiotic stresses. Such GMO plants will reduce the need of mutagenic and carcinogenic pesticides and can help in creating a cleaner environment. Moreover, the use of recombinant microorganisms for bioremediation is a constant and growing need to clean land fills, sewage and carbon-based fuel spills. Also,

GMOs are currently used to fortify food and feed with essential vitamins and amino acids and plant-made pharmaceuticals create a more efficient way of getting medicines to patients.

Opportunities for Innovation and Global Integration

A strong partnership between industry, academia, and government is essential for the development of a successful biotechnology sector. Developed countries actively encourage and facilitate technology transfer from the academic research institutions as well as helping to promote investment into biotechnology companies. According to the 2006 study published by the Biotechnology Industry Organization, there are five components essential for bioscience industry development:

1. Academic Integration and Technology Transfer
2. Specialized Facilities
3. Capital Formation
4. Educated Work Force
5. Supportive Public Policy

Academia Research, Integration, and Technology Transfer

In order to sustain invention and innovation, continual partnerships between academic research centers and companies is critical. The successful transfer of government funded research for commercialization is the key to the long-term viability of the industry. Although technology transfer has been recognized by universities and the government, there are other objectives that are equally important to consider. Universities create and share information through publication and public disclosure. Government agencies appropriate funds for basic research and broker fiscal and intellectual assets for the public good. Successful technology transfer identifies ways to create appropriate conversion of public resources to private enterprise while hopefully improving the economic prosperity for the country.

Currently the predominant academic clusters in the Kingdom are housed at the Jordan University of Science and Technology Princess Haya Biotechnology Center and the Higher Council of Science and Technology National Biotechnology Center. To date, there is one transfer of academic research into the private sector. MONOJO, a start-up company producing monoclonal antibodies was spun out of the Higher Council's National Biotechnology Center.

Public Institutions with Applied Sciences and Biotechnology Programs

The pace of knowledge creation has transformed the research process to the point where no one scientist or institution can sufficiently conduct wholly independent research programs. The U.S. makes this relationship a reality as the central initiator of the collaboration between academic investigators and industry researchers in the decades since the passage of the Bayh-Dole Act of 1980.

> **The Bayh-Dole Act of 1980** was a landmark piece of federal legislation that for the first time allowed universities to actively pursue the transfer of government funded research into the marketplace. This act has been copied by every nation interested in moving university invention into market innovation. The Association of University Technology Managers (AUTUM) in 2005 estimated that since the Bayh-Dole Act became law, more than 1,500 technology companies have been created as a result of the transfer of university research to the private sector.

The standard definition of technology transfer in the US and developed countries is the transfer of the innovation from academia to the private sector. In the U.S. there are systems in place that transition innovation into profit. In Jordan, the definition of technology transfer is bringing technology from the West to the developing countries. This concept of tech transfer within Jordan has the opportunity to be defined by the standard developed definition and brought into process. Jordan's strength is the competitive education curriculums and research institutions – this is a major expense in the United States and can be an attractive draw for Jordan.

Below is a list of biotechnology programs within the academic institutions of Jordan:

The National Center for Biotechnology

Website: www.ncb.gov.jo

The National Center for Biotechnology is a virtual center housed under the Higher Council of Science and Technology. This Center's vision is to catalyze development in the field of biotechnology. This virtual institute functions to support cooperation and the work of scientists in their own institutions. The plan of the Center is to act as a model for sister Institutions in the Arab World.

The Center is charged with the following tasks:

1. Identifying the national capabilities, potential and activities, in the field of Biotechnology, and coordinating and developing such activities at the different scientific centers and institutions, as well as building the database required.
2. Supporting the Applied Scientific Research in the field of Biotechnology.
3. Nurturing and supporting the establishment of Biotechnology products based enterprises.
4. Increasing the number of patents, and supporting inventions and innovation in Biotechnology.

The Center has produced a database creating a voluntary Scientists Network on-line. A scientist can volunteer their specialty, expertise, and publicize what equipment that is in their possession. The list of scientists classified and referenced are public on the website, divided into ten groups: Commercial Production of Enzymes and Antibodies, Agricultural, Environmental, Natural Products, Veterinary Science, Testing, Genetic Engineering, Bioinformatics, Microbiology, and other biotechnologies. The Center also publicly provides data on grants provided by the Higher Council and the location of specialized equipment in-country.

In the developed world the line between basic and applied research has all but disappeared. Universities in the West are now requiring their researchers to patent their discoveries and inventions and are encouraging their professors to go into the marketplace. In Jordan, this approach is still in its infancy. The low level of spending on scientific research can, at least in part, be attributed to the fact that Jordan does not see the benefits from investing in research.

Princess Haya Biotechnology Center
Jordan University of Science and Technology (JUST)

Website: http://ejust.just.edu.jo/Center/PHBC/index.aspx?PID=1&PNAME=Mission

The Department of Biotechnology and Genetic Engineering at JUST was established in 1999. Dr. Wajih Owais, JUST President and Dr. Said Jaradat, Director of the Princess Biotechnology Center wanted to create an environment in which Jordan could become competitive with the growth of the industry. JUST focuses on investment into human resources, training and preparing students for careers in the field.

The Center operates on an annual budget of $300,000 USD per year. The obtained funding is primarily from JUST, and several grant sources including the US Department of STATE. Funding is obtained for forensics and DNA identification for unidentified bodies in Iraq. And, scientists from all over the region come to JUST for series of training and educational seminars.

The curriculum at the Department of Biotechnology and Genetic Engineering spans a broad range of basic sciences, from Microbiology, Biochemistry, Genetics, Molecular biology, Plant physiology, and Immunology. JUST contains an FDA biological controlled laboratory. The Department consists of 12 faculty members and 516 undergraduate students.

The center has recently expanded its activity beyond the national borders and established scientific cooperation with Arab and other countries. Cooperation is underway with forensic medicine institute in Iraq, the Saint Joseph University in Lebanon, and the Hamdan Bin Rashid Organization for Excellence in the UAE. In addition, the center hosts a number of graduate students from Saudi Arabia. Furthermore, there are a number of scientific cooperation agreements with the Human Genetics Center at the University of Humboldt in Germany and The Forensic Medicine Center at the University of Western Australia and Saint Lawrence College in New York.

The center aims to increase awareness of the importance of biotechnology and research in order to help solve the large number of medical and health problems suffered by Jordanian people. In addition, the center seeks to actively participate in creating an advanced biotech industry on a firm scientific and technological base. For this reason the center has the short term goal for this year of preparing an Oracle database that should become a nucleus for the most advanced center for biotechnology and bioinformatics in the Arab region and will help the center achieve its long term goals. In addition, the center hopes to establish a virology research unit this year in light of the pressing need for such a unit in the Kingdom created by the recent rise of incidents in of the Bird Flu and other viral infections in adjacent countries.

Dr. Jaradat presented a number of challenges within Jordan concerning ethical practices and genetic counseling. Due to the population groups in Jordan, certain genetic disease statistics are unusually high. Five percent of the population carries Cystic Fibrosis. And, with technology being obtained from outside of the country, questionable practices are on the radar. Overall, this Institute appears to be a go to Center in the region and has the most consistent international partnerships of any particular body.

King Hussein Cancer and Biotechnology Institute (KHCBI)

KHCBI is a not-for-profit non governmental organization established in 2006 as an initiative of King Abdullah II Fund for Development in concordance with His Majesty King Abdullah II's vision of transforming Jordan into a regional and international center providing cancer patients with an internationally competitive environment. Dr. Samir Khleif is directing this initiative, receiving grants for a Phase I study of the regulatory infrastructure needed in Jordan to draw biotechnology companies into Jordan to conduct Clinical Trials. The study is being conducted by the Research Triangle Institute of North Carolina (RTI). The RTI team is currently researching the legal framework and providing Best Practice recommendations for the biotechnology sector. RTI will present the first draft to KHCBI at the end of October, 2007 and conclude the report by the end of December, 2007.

University of Jordan

Website: www.ju.edu.jo/Faculties/Faculties_Agriculture/agriculture_departments.html

The University of Jordan has a number of applied sciences programs in the following departments: Department of Biology, Department of Agriculture: Department of Horticulture and Crop Science, Department of Animal Production , Department of Nutrition and Food Technology, Department of Land, Water and Environment, Department of Plant Protection. Focusing primarily on agriculture, this University has a number of plant breeding initiatives underway related to the Mediterranean climate. Little international collaboration is known as there is an official ban on agriculture biotechnology within the Kingdom.

Hashemite University
Department of Biological Sciences and Biotechnology

Website: http://www.hu.edu.jo/Inside/Academics/Sciences/biology.asp

The Department of Biological Sciences was established in 1995. The department offers a Bachelor of Science degree in Biological Sciences and Biotechnology. The department has a limited number of programs in which distinguished students can continue their study for postgraduate studies and scientific research. The biotechnology program focuses on applications of the biosciences to human and animal health, agricultural, environmental and industrial problems. Courses includes genetic engineering technology, basic sciences such as biochemistry, microbiology, molecular biology and immunology, applied sciences such as industrial biotechnology and laboratory techniques, recombinant DNA methods, and commercial biotechnology. In 2005/2006, 91 students were enrolled in the Departments Biology program and 70 students were enrolled in the Biotechnology Program.

Philadelphia University

Website: http://www.philadelphia.edu.jo/biotech/

The Department of Biotechnology and genetic engineering at Philadelphia University was established in 2000. The University created this Department in response to the growing need for specialists in technological fields.

The department offers a Bachelor of Science Degree in Biotechnology and Genetic Engineering. These include molecular biology, recombinant DNA, protein engineering, immunology, genetics, animal and plant tissue culture, plant science, environmental science, microbiology, biochemistry and computing. The Department is planning to introduce postgraduate studies in the next few years. The University reported that graduates in Biotechnology and Genetic Engineering go into the following fields:

- Research Centers
- Specialty Hospitals
- Agricultural Centers
- Ministry of Health
- Pharmaceutical Industry
- Forensic Medicine
- Environmental Protection Agencies
- Biotechnology Marketing
- Animal Husbandry

The majority of the students that do pursue biotechnology jobs in the private sector leave the country for high paying jobs in specific fields. Both the UAE and India are attractive draws for Jordanian graduates.

Specialized Facilities

Biotech companies have two characteristics that distinguish them from young companies in other technology industries. First, bioscience firms are subject to a longer and more costly federally mandated oversight process. In the United States in 2006, this protracted R&D regimen was averaging 10-12 years and could cost more than $1 billion to get a human drug product approved. Second, unlike other technology industries, biotech companies are required to conduct research in highly specialized and government inspected facilities. The specialization required in these research facilities make them some of the most expensive business real estate to develop. Many Universities in the U.S. are now investing in the development of specialized facilities to serve as incubators for small and emerging biotech companies.

In Jordan, the private sector has independent investments into clean rooms and compliance with ISO 9000 certified standards. Medical device manufacturing companies in Jordan comply with these standards, along with incubator companies out of the Higher Council. The public sector has a varied degree of standards with the Princess Haya Biotechnology Center at JUST having international recognition and standardization.

Capital Formation

The need for early-stage funding for bioscience companies is essential. Locating funding to underwrite innovative research is an on-going challenge to companies. Small startup companies with high quality research and personnel look for the vital funds needed to get up and running where as established bioscience companies require funding to invest in additional infrastructure and clinical research to move products into the marketplace.

There are active Venture Capital Firms in Jordan, focusing on energy and water related start-ups and technology. However, when meeting with prominent investors in the biotechnology arena, most prefer holding their investments in funds or companies directly in the United States.

As for funding for academic research, this is the essential component in order to launch an attractive biotechnology cluster. In the late 1990's, hundreds of millions of dollars were funneled into U.S. State Universities. Funding came from tobacco settlements. Universities were awarded this funding from State Governments and channeled it into research and development. When observing the high rates of lung cancer and other related cancers in Jordan, and the lack of capacity to support the health crises, a review of the cost of cigarettes in Jordan, and an opportunity to create a funding mechanism in which to create R&D opportunities is encouraged.

Educated Workforce

Countries that possess a high-quality labor force are attractive to any industry. Because the skills required for many aspects of commercialization are high, a continuing flow of educated (Ph.D., MS, BS, AA) and technically trained workers is essential if a country desires to enhance the industry's presence. Conversely, if a country does not have an indigenous industry, it is difficult to retain those individuals receiving science and technical degrees from the country's universities.

Upon King Abdullah II's request, a steering committee was formed back in March 2005 from visionaries in Jordan to set research and development priorities based on the country's present human and natural resources. As several Universities offer biotechnology programs in Jordan, the first task recommended is to conduct a human resource study of the brain power in Jordan. Within the study, identify the skill gaps between graduates of science from local universities and requirements of the industry. In various interviews, a notable comment by a prominent pharmaceutical manufacturing company stated that in the process of acquiring a biotechnology manufacturing company in Germany, they are deciding to maintain the location in Germany as they believe the learning curve for training Jordanians is too steep.

Supportive Public Policy for Biotechnology Development

The need for a stable and supportive public policy framework is vital to industry firms large and small. It is almost impossible for any country or region to ignore the need for selective incentives to either hold existing biotech companies or attract new enterprises. In addition, efforts to restrict certain types of research within the sector can impact the ability to promote other areas of industry development.

The Research Triangle Institute (RTI) of North Carolina, located in an internationally renowned biotech cluster, is operating on a grant through the King Hussein Cancer and Biotechnology Institute to assess all legal and regulatory frameworks of Jordan in order to develop Best Practice Guidelines to create greater receptivity for the international biotechnology industry to enter Jordan.

RTI is evaluating the following laws and comparing Best Practice models with the U.S., EU, Ireland, and Singapore in order to create guidelines for the Kingdom of Jordan. This Best Practices Model shall be completed by the end of 2007. These laws only apply to the biotechnology sector related to healthcare.

Jordan Laws Affecting the Biotechnology Industry

Law of Higher Health Council* Law of Pharmacists Association*Clinical Studies Law

Public Health Law*Ordinance Licensing Private*Medical Laboratories*Higher Council of Science and Technology Law*Ordinances of the National Biotechnology Center

Drug and Pharmacy Law*Ordinance on Testing of Drugs*Ordinance on Licensing Private Medical Laboratories*Principles and requirements for licensing parties and accreditation of laboratories*Public Health Law regarding drug ingredients*Ordinance on testing of drugs*Principles for importing and circulating drug supplies*

Art 49 of Public Health Law on waste disposal from laboratories, vaccines, drug factories, health research centers only*Environmental Health*Copyright Law*Patent Law*Article 20 of the Labor Law on treatment of inventions by employees*Registration of Drugs*Registration Procedures, Article 14*"Contractual" production of registered drug*Pricing Procedures*Clinical Studies Law

Upon conclusion of these Best Practice Guidelines, coordination with the King Hussein Cancer and Biotechnology Institute in order for active and consistent implementation is needed.

Bioethics

With the distribution, use, and exploration of technology within the country, there is an absence of ethical compliance and practices. The Director of the Princess Haya Biotechnology Center has encountered a number of questionable practices and as a key focal point in the country and in the region, is considered a reference point when ethics are in question. Currently, there are no ethical guidelines or discussions and accountability related to biotechnology. A priority for this Center is a need for an ethical discussion when using the technology and its applications.

The Biotechnology Industry Organization (BIO), the leading trade association in the biotechnology industry has created an active committee, adopting a Statement of Ethical Principles in order to ensure biotechnology is used for the betterment of humankind and not abused. If SABEQ decides to support initiatives advancing this sector, incorporating bioethics into any programs is strongly recommended.

Agriculture

Globally, the agriculture biotechnology sector is a much different business model than the healthcare biotechnology sector. Ag biotech is dominated by a handful of multinational players that tend to have public private sector initiatives set up with leading universities, USAID, and major markets. There is overlap within the sectors such as nutriceuticals, plant-made pharmaceuticals, and animal biotech applications. With Jordan's population growth and limited resources, dedicated research to the needs of improving the agriculture sector can be applied to the fruits and vegetable industry. As referenced in the academic listing, the majority of agriculture research, plant breeding needs is done at the University of Jordan. There is a great deal of interest and ideas on R&D opportunities, but the market does not support many of them. R&D investment for the future on Jordan's largest vegetable crops such as tomatoes, zucchini, and eggplant could be a potential focus. That includes no significant market resistance to GM as would be the case for exported vegetables to Europe or sensitive Middle East markets such as Saudia Arabia.

Within the private sector, Seminis, a vegetable and fruit seed company has been recently acquired by Monsanto. Seminis has distribution and marketing offices in Jordan and is consider a sleeper for potential biotech activity in the future. Syngenta has a significant R&D center in the north of Jordan.

USAID Global Biotechnology Programs

USAID has an active worldwide agriculture biotechnology program, focusing on Africa and South Asia. There are three major areas the Agency works in with respect to biotech:

1. Technology Development: Development of improved crops and animal vaccines/diagnostics
2. Policy/Regulatory/Biosafety policy: To address environmental safety, food safety, and trade issues. These activities range from assisting with national policy and regulations to training of regulators
3. Outreach: Public relations, communication, and marketing needs to the public, media, policy makers, farmers to sensitize stakeholders to support development and implementation of policy.

Policy Threat

In 2004, a governmental intra-agency working group developed recommendations for a policy protocol for approvals of agriculture biotechnology for imports and local growth. To date, there is an official ban on agriculture biotechnology development. Once the recommendations were made to the Ministers of Agriculture, Environment, Health, and JFDA, no official action was taken. The document could not be accessed for publication of this report. There is no public commercial agriculture biotechnology is taking place.

Industrial, Energy, and Environment

In conversations with USAID-SABEQ, Biotech Compass was specifically requested to explore uses of biotechnology applications within the industrial, environmental, energy, and garment and textiles sector.

There is activity within industrial biotechnology applications but the networks were not as transparent, and the business models for investment are different. There is a venture capital firm operating in Jordan dedicated to the investment of start-ups related to energy and water. Upon request, and in reviewing the garment sector, the amount of water consumed, and the cost applications for treating water were quite high. Instead, Infilco Degremont, the multinational water treatment company under contract with USAID suggested that water be hauled to their IDI plant at Wadi Ma'in for treatment of the prescribed chemicals.

Private Sector

The level in which the private sector is active in the Kingdom varies. A number of biotechnology companies distribute products in the Kingdom, companies such as Amgen and Genzyme have operations or relationships with Drugstores. Individual Drugstores distribute biotechnology and biopharmaceutical products and requested that Biotech Compass identify specific biotech products for them and introduce them to small and medium sized FDA-approved biotechnology companies in the United States. Drugstores are interested and willing to distribute biotechnology products.

Jordan pharmaceutical manufacturers are traveling in search of opportunities to manufacture biopharmaceutical processes. Jordan has a strong connection with the German biotech industry and with German's biotechnology sector in a cash poor state, a Jordan Manufacturer is in the process of acquiring a biotechnology company with the plan to maintain the manufacturing facility in Germany. When asked the reasons why to not house production facilities in Jordan, the response was that the learning curve for training in equipment and processes would be too exhaustive.

Communication and Marketing

In interviews throughout the academic community, it is evident that there is competition for recognition and funding and a lack of transparency of the mechanisms and activity currently existing for scientific advancement. In order for the sector to move forward, creation of a system in which there is communication on activities and projects, resources in which biotechnology programs can identify collaboration or apply for grant funding.

Jordan has the opportunity to increase international recognition of their existing needs and capabilities. The Middle East region is second in worldwide market growth over the next 5 years, next to China and South Asia. In addition, consumer reports within the multinational brand-name pharmaceutical industry state that Arabs prefer brand name and innovative products. This results in opportunity for growth within the biotechnology and pharmaceutical sectors.

Marketing these opportunities, the existing academic system, and the Jordan Niche to the biotechnology industry would attract small and medium sized enterprises looking for partnerships and collaboration.

Israel

Recognizing the promotion of Jordan Israel collaboration in economic development and acknowledging the active biotechnology industry in Israel, Biotech Compass identified an Arab Israeli Biotechnology Incubator located in Israel and reviewed the Israeli Biotech Incubator System.

New Generation Technology Biotechnology Incubator

Website: www.ngtnazareth.com

New Generation Technology (NGT) Technological Incubator in Nazareth, Israel Founded in July, 2002, NGT is a technological incubator located in Nazareth. NGT is part of the National Incubator Program that supports and encourages entrepreneurial projects in the fields of technology and biotechnology with guidance and support from the Office of the Chief Scientist of the Ministry of Industry and Trade. As such, it is also the first incubator of its type to be owned by Jewish and Israeli Arabs businessmen. In addition, NGT aims to encourage entrepreneurs from both the Jewish and Arab sectors of the Israeli population.

The NGT facilities are located in a modern 860 square meter building in industrial area of Nazareth.

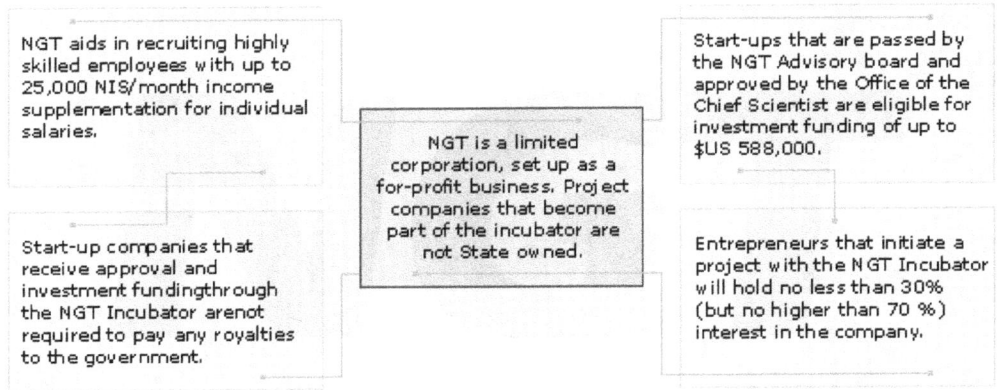

In meeting these entrepreneurs and staff supporting this biotechnology incubator, several scientists expressed interest in research collaboration with Jordan, focusing on research that affects the Arab population.

In conclusion is a list of recommendations that SABEQ can undertake in order to support the advancement of the sector. From support for funding mechanisms for R&D, to assessing the policy needs and linking Jordan to US institutions, there is a number of opportunities for SABEQ to advance the sector. Specifically, Dr. Samir Khleif requested two studies to be conducted in order to promote the King Hussein Cancer and Biotechnology Institute.

Recommendations

In summarizing the existing capabilities of Jordan, the opportunities of advancing the biotechnology sector, requests by leader's in the Jordan biotech community, and SABEQ's scope, the following is a list of ideas in which SABEQ can adopt to further support this sector:

1. An evaluation of the human resources in the Kingdom. Conduct a study of the brainpower in Jordan related to the scientific field. For example, how many Jordanians have a bachelor's in biology, bachelors in biotechnology, master's in chemistry, any specialties, and so on. An estimated 600 students graduate each year with degrees in biotechnology from Jordan's academic institutions. This public study would be a valuable resource to the King Hussein Biotechnology Institute and was per the suggestion of Dr. Samir Khleif. In addition, this study would publicize the brain power of Jordan, thus attracting global biotechnology companies to develop partnerships with local incubator companies in order to collaborate on R&D. Adding to the study would be the need to assess the level of knowledge of practical skills and expertise in science graduates in the Kingdom.
2. Jordan Niche: Assess the unique characteristics of the population and biodiversity of Jordan. This was another recommendation provided by Dr. Samir Khleif and supported by Dr. Wajih Owais and Dr. Said Jaradat. A document examining the special properties of Jordan could then be used as a marketing tool for global biotechs to develop partnerships with local research institutions.
3. Assess all international aid health projects, agriculture, projects, and aid projects on-going in Jordan. Cross reference their needs and create a mechanism in which to provide this information to the biotechnology industry.
4. Provide the previous three documents to the Biotechnology Industry Organization (BIO), using BIO as a vehicle to market Jordan to the global biotechnology community.
5. Creation of a High-Level Dialogue: Create a distinguished committee of Jordanians involved in the biotechnology field, whom meet regularly either monthly or bi-monthly to exchange ideas and needs with SABEQ. This would be a moderated discussion in which the moderator would be responsible for the follow through regarding the agreed upon next steps.
6. Create an Arab Scientist Collaborative Network between Arab scientists in Jordan and Israel.
7. House a focal point of published funding resources, identifying grant opportunities for Jordanian scientists and facilitate and coordinate global exposure. Establish relationships with the Gates Foundation, Rockefeller Institute, Pew Initiative and all other non-profit arms that provide funding for academic research. Link these relationships with the Jordan Universities and establish relationships with U.S. Universities that are interested in Jordan Niche areas. This integrated website could also list Jordan's scientific research and reference scientist's independent research.
8. Consistent and repetitive integration of Jordanian scientists in global partnering and investment conferences. BIO-Europe is a specific global partnering event that meets twice yearly. Jordanian scientists could identify R&D opportunities and joint ventures with small and medium sized biotechs and multinational pharma companies.
9. Resurrect the intra-agency working group led by JFDA recommendations on the regulations of R&D of agriculture biotechnology
10. Integrate the existing USAID Global Agriculture Programs into Jordan through SABEQ.
11. Academic Funding: Create a Center for R&D, tax cigarettes or locate another in country capital resource and dedicate the funding to biotech R&D. This was a common practice in the United States, and a catalyst for innovation in academic research institutions in the late 1990's.

12. Further the existing Master and Ph.D. exchange programs in which Jordanian students that have received a Bachelors Degree in Biotechnology may attend a U.S. University to further research and focus specifically to issues related to the needs of Jordan.

13. Connectivity: Jordan has a virtual National Biotechnology Centre however, several of the biotechnology programs are isolated in independent pockets. In order to continue advancing the sector, facilitating a face-to-face linking point.

14. Laboratory Environments: For R&D in biotechnology, laboratory specifications and equipment are needed. The Princess Haya Biotechnology Center is in the process of achieving international accreditation. Assist in the completion of this accreditation. Identify where other laboratories in the Kingdom can receive a similar heightened status.

Reference Documents

Biotechnology Industry Organization and Council of State Bioscience Associations

State Legislative Best Practices in Support of Bioscience Industry Development, Battelle Report November, 2006

King Abdullah II International Advisory Board White Paper

National Life Sciences Research Development and Biotechnology Promotion Initiative in Jordan, 2005

New Generation Technology Biotechnology Incubator, Nazareth, Israel

United Nations International Development Organization

The Biotechnology Sector in Jordan Final report: Mission to Jordan, 2004

Interviews

Advanced Medical Industries (AMI): Saher Al-Nabulsi

Burgan Drugstores: Basel Burgan, CEO

Drug Importer's Association: Thamer Obeidat, Director General

Hikma Pharmaceuticals

Higher Council for Science and Technology Dr. Walid Al-Turk, Chairman

Pharmaceutical Manufacturers Association (PhRMA) Dr. Samir Mansour, Representative

Infilco Degremont International (IDI): Evan Claytor, Engineer

Jordan Pharmaceutical Association

Jordan Pharmaceutical Manufacturers Association Dr. Hanan Sbhoul, Secretary General

Jordan University: Professors and Consultants

Jordan University of Science and Technology (JUST): Dr. Wajih Owais, President

King Hussein Cancer and Biotechnology Institute: Dr. Samir Khleif, Director General

MONOJO Monoclonal Antibodies Company: Penlopa Ahmed, CEO

Monsanto Company: Warren M. Strauss, V.P. of Global Operations

New Generation Technology (NGT): Nasri Saad, Director of Business Development

Prometheus Consulting: Dr. Val Giddings, CEO

Princess Haya Biotechnology Center, JUST: Dr. Said Jaradat, Director

USAID Global Biotechnology Programs: Josette Lewis, Director

USAID SABEQ Staff: Component Four

USAID Jordan Women Health Project: Dr. Rita Leavell, M.D.

Addendum 1 – USAID Biotech Brochure – See separate document

 **AGRICULTURE**

FROM THE AMERICAN PEOPLE

Biotechnology

Modern molecular biology offers powerful new tools for improving agricultural productivity, environmental quality, and the nutritional quality of staple foods. At the same time, some applications of biotechnology raise concerns of safety, access, and equity in benefits. The science of biotechnology is helping to guide more precise crop and livestock breeding efforts, to diagnose crops and livestock diseases, to develop more effective livestock vaccines, and to engineer plants resistant to diseases and pests. The goal of USAID is to assist developing countries in building the framework for decision-making that will facilitate access to these opportunities the science holds and will ensure the safe and effective application of this technology.

USAID supports development of biotechnology as a component of our strategy to increase agricultural productivity and economic growth. Biotechnology compliments other USAID agricultural research programs in breeding, natural resources management, integrated pest management, and post-harvest technologies. In 1989, USAID launched an innovative approach to biotechnology, one that integrates technology development with the establishment of the policy frameworks necessary for the safe and effective application of the technology in developing countries. In addition, this strategy harnesses the private sector's investment and expertise to further the goals of public research in developing countries.

USAID has recently expanded its support for biotechnology, reflecting the increasing demand in developing countries to be part of this new scientific revolution and to build their capacity to ensure the safe application of biotechnology. The Agency's Collaborative Agricultural Biotechnology Initiative (CABIO) provides a comprehensive strategy for technology development, management, and decision-making through a variety of programs. CABIO links investments at the national, regional and global levels.

These collaborative programs engage the expertise of U.S. and developing country universities, the private sector, non-governmental organizations, the Consultative Group on International Agricultural Research (CGIAR), and other international institutions.

The goals of the programs include:

> develop technologies targeted to small farmers in developing countries,

build scientific capacity through short and long term training,
enable public research systems to address regulatory and intellectual property rights issues as they move research forward,
develop and strengthen the systems to regulate the safety of biotechnology,
fund environmental research to inform risk assessment and management of biotechnology.

To promote the safe application of biotechnology, and to ensure compliance with national and international policies, USAID has implemented the following biotech policies and practices:

USAID will not support the transfer of bioengineered materials intended for planting without the host government's explicit advanced informed consent. Grantees and contractors must comply with national and international laws applicable to biotechnology research and testing. Further, USAID conducts an independent assessment of the potential environmental or safety risks before supporting the transfer of materials intended for direct release into the environment.
USAID supports activities to build the capacity of governments to evaluate and manage the safety of bioengineered products. In addition to regulatory policy development and training, USAID also supports efforts by developing country scientists and policy makers to address local public outreach on issues of biotechnology.
USAID supports environmental research to address potential risks to biodiversity from bioengineered products in the specific environmental and agro-ecological environments of developing countries.

The ultimate objective of USAID's investments in biotechnology is to provide farmers with improved crop varieties and livestock technology to increase productivity. We work to develop staple food crops that will fight off devastating diseases that contribute to food insecurity and low productivity in Africa, such as insect-resistant cowpeas, disease-resistant bananas, and disease-resistant cassava, the staple foods of many poor in Africa. Biotechnology also provides the opportunity to increase nutritional quality of crops to address the debilitating impacts of malnutrition, supporting the development of Golden Rice for Asia, golden mustard for India, and vitamin A enhanced maize for Africa.